DINOSAUR DAYS

STEGOSAURUS
The Plated Dinosaur

Benchmark Books
Marshall Cavendish Corporation
99 White Plains Road
Tarrytown, New York 10591-9001

Scientific consultant:
Rolf Johnson, Associate Curator of Paleontology;
Director, Science Media Center; Milwaukee Public Museum

Library of Congress Cataloging-in-Publication
Riehecky, Janet, date.
Stegosaurus : the plated dinosaur/ Janet Riehecky ;
illustrated by Susan Tolonen.
p.   cm -- (Dinosaur days)
Includes bibliographical references (p.   ) and index.
Summary: Describes a day in the life of the plant-eating stegosaurus, noting
its behavior, environment, and physical characteristics.
ISBN 0-7614-0604-2
1. Stegosaurus--Juvenile literature. [1. Stegosaurus. 2. Dinosaurs.]
I. Tolonen, Susan, date, ill. II. Title. III. Series: Riehecky, Janet, date. Dinosaur Days.
QE862.065R54   1998   567.915'3--dc21   96-49419   CIP   AC

Printed in the United States of America

1 3 5 7 8 6 4 2

DINOSAUR DAYS

STEGOSAURUS
The Plated Dinosaur

WRITTEN BY JANET RIEHECKY
ILLUSTRATED BY SUSAN TOLONEN

BENCHMARK BOOKS

MARSHALL CAVENDISH
NEW YORK

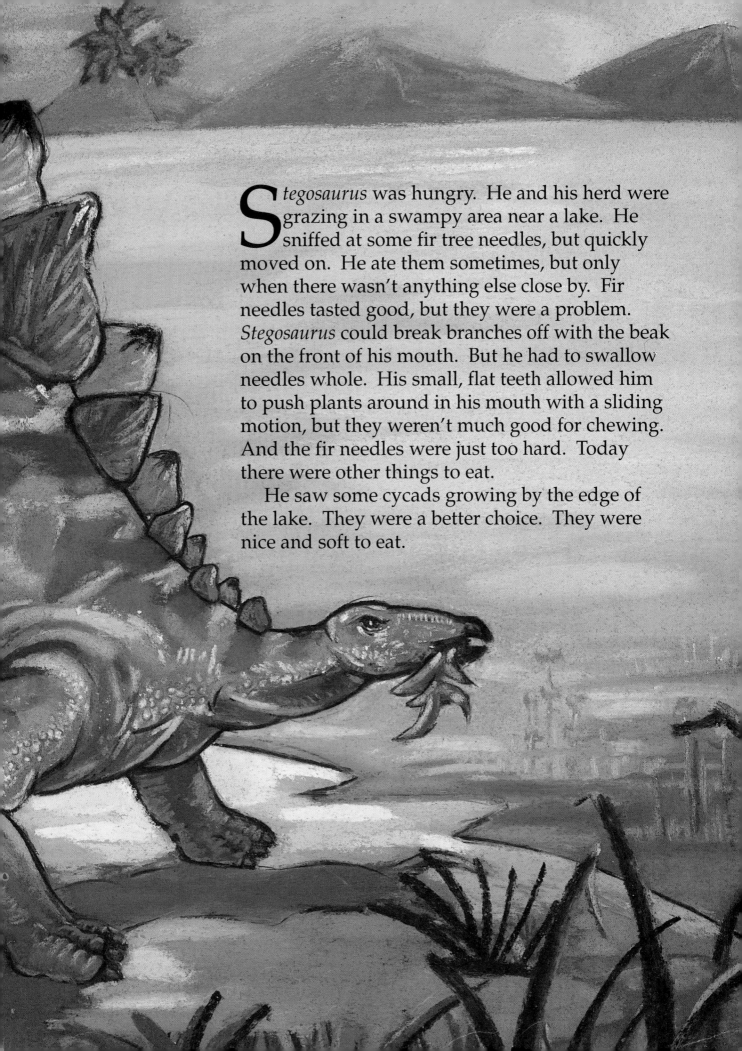

Stegosaurus was hungry. He and his herd were grazing in a swampy area near a lake. He sniffed at some fir tree needles, but quickly moved on. He ate them sometimes, but only when there wasn't anything else close by. Fir needles tasted good, but they were a problem. *Stegosaurus* could break branches off with the beak on the front of his mouth. But he had to swallow needles whole. His small, flat teeth allowed him to push plants around in his mouth with a sliding motion, but they weren't much good for chewing. And the fir needles were just too hard. Today there were other things to eat.

He saw some cycads growing by the edge of the lake. They were a better choice. They were nice and soft to eat.

  Stegosaurus swallowed some cycad fronds. His herd was close by.
There were more than a hundred dinosaurs in his herd, and they were all
eating, too. *Stegosaurus* made sure to stay close. It was safer that way.
Meat-eating dinosaurs seemed less likely to attack animals in a herd.
  Across the lake, *Stegosaurus* could see a herd of apatosaurs. The
apatosaurs were each bigger than a house, but they didn't worry him.
Apatosaurs only ate plants. And most of the time their meal was the
leaves from the tops of the tallest trees. *Stegosaurus* couldn't reach those
anyway. He was only 11 feet (3.3 meters) tall. And that was at his hips.
His head and mouth were only a few feet from the ground.

Stegosaurus ate plants most of the morning. By midday, though, he was getting hot. The plates on his back usually helped Stegosaurus feel cooler. The heat in his body traveled through the blood in the skin on his plates and then out into the air. But sometimes that wasn't enough. Then it felt good to get out of the sun. He moved into the woods, under the shade of the trees. Some of the other stegosaurs followed him.

Stegosaurus nibbled on some ferns and then moved to a tree with low branches. He ate a few of the leaves. Then he reared up, standing on just his back legs. He placed his front feet against the tree trunk and his tail on the ground to balance himself. Then he reached for some of the higher leaves.

After a while, *Stegosaurus* felt cooler and decided to move back to the lake. He waded a few feet into the water to take a drink. Nearby he noticed a log floating mostly under the water. He didn't pay any attention to it—until it started to move toward him and opened its mouth! It wasn't a log. It was a crocodile!

The crocodile was nine
feet (2.7 meters) long, with a
mouthful of long, sharp teeth.
Stegosaurus backed quickly
away. Even though he was much
bigger than the crocodile, he was
still in trouble. If the crocodile bit his leg,
it could hurt him so badly he wouldn't be able to
walk well. And if he fell down, the crocodile could drag him into the
water and kill him. Even if he got away, he would have a problem
keeping up with the herd. Then a meat-eating dinosaur could get him.

This time *Stegosaurus* was lucky. He got out of the way quickly
enough that the crocodile decided to go after a large fish instead.

Stegosaurus began to eat some
ferns that grew near the lake. He ate
one mouthful after another after another.
Stegosaurus could take only very small
bites most of the time, because his mouth
was so small compared to his huge body.
And he had a very big stomach to fill.

Stegosaurus finished one plant and
moved to the next. He and his herd
moved slowly, eating all the time. They
were headed for a special place—the
nesting grounds.

14

15

The nesting grounds were on the shore of a lake. When they got there, after a long journey, only the females went down to the nesting grounds. On the long, sandy beach, they each used their feet and the tips of their snouts to make holes in the ground.

These were their nests. In the nests, they laid large, oval eggs in circles. They covered the eggs with leafy plants, such as ferns. As the plants decayed, they would help keep the eggs warm until they hatched.

The females returned to the herd after they laid their eggs. When the babies hatched, they would be on their own. They would have to find their own food and stay away from meat eaters.

The babies looked pretty much like their parents, except that they had only small bumps instead of plates on their backs. The plates would grow in as the babies got older. When the babies grew big enough, about the size of a large dog, they would be able to join a herd. The herds moved slowly, but they still wouldn't wait for any dinosaur that couldn't keep up.

The herd moved on after the females laid their eggs. As they traveled, they ate almost every low-growing plant they passed. They liked to stop in wet, marshy areas. Most meat-eating dinosaurs didn't like places like this. But they never missed a chance to fill their large bellies.

As they passed a river, *Stegosaurus* found a clump of ferns. He began to nibble on them. The ferns tasted so good, he didn't notice that his herd was moving farther and farther away. But an *Allosaurus* did.

The *Allosaurus* waited patiently, hiding behind a tree. He watched *Stegosaurus* carefully. Soon *Stegosaurus* moved to a clump of ferns closer to *Allosaurus*. *Allosaurus* decided to attack.

With a bellow, *Allosaurus* charged. He kicked at *Stegosaurus*, trying to slash his side with the huge claws on his feet.

Stegosaurus didn't try to run away. He knew he couldn't run faster than *Allosaurus*. He turned his back on *Allosaurus* and lifted his tail. Some of his strongest muscles were in his tail. And he had four sharp spikes on the end of it. Whack! He hit *Allosaurus* in his thigh.

Allosaurus bellowed in pain, but he didn't give up. He jumped to the side, away from *Stegosaurus*'s tail, and tried again to slash him. As he lunged forward, the tip of one of his claws scratched *Stegosaurus*'s side. The cut began to bleed.

24

Stegosaurus knew he had to get away quickly. Again he swung his tail at *Allosaurus*. This time he caught *Allosaurus* in his knee joint. *Allosaurus* fell over with a loud crash! *Stegosaurus* didn't wait to see if *Allosaurus* could get up again. He hurried after his herd.

Stegosaurus caught up with his herd in a marsh. There were lots of tasty plants nearby. But before he started eating, *Stegosaurus* rolled around in the mud. The mud caked over the cut on *Stegosaurus*'s side. It would help the cut heal and protect it from insects. *Stegosaurus* wiggled around a few minutes more, just because it felt good.

Then, he began munching the plants.

SOME FACTS ABOUT . . . STEGOSAURUS

Physical Appearance

Stegosaurus is one of the most unusual dinosaurs. It grew to about ten to twelve feet tall (3.1 to 3.7 meters) at its hips and about twenty-five to thirty feet long (7.5 to 9.2 meters) when fully grown. It weighed about two to three tons (1.8 to 2.7 metric tons). Its back legs were twice as long as its front legs, causing its back to curve like a slide. There were five toes on its front feet and three toes (with part of a fourth) on its back. But what was most unusual about *Stegosaurus* was the diamond-shaped plates on its back.

Scientists argue about how the plates were arranged on *Stegosaurus*'s back. Some think there was just one row of plates. Others think there were two rows, with the plates arranged in pairs. Still others think there were two rows, but with the plates alternating. The largest plates were over its hips. These could be thirty inches (seventy-six centimeters) high and thirty-one inches (seventy-eight centimeters) wide.

Scientists used to think the plates on *Stegosaurus*'s back were for protection. They thought the plates lay flat on its back, like shingles on a roof. (The name *Stegosaurus* means "roofed lizard.") But even if that were true, the plates wouldn't be very good protection. They could cover only part of *Stegosaurus*'s back. There would be nothing to protect its sides and belly. Most scientists now think that the plates were used either to attract a mate or to control the *Stegosaurus*'s body temperature. Like a radiator, the plates gave off heat carried to them from *Stegosaurus*'s body, thus cooling the body.

Lifestyle

For many years, *Stegosaurus* was thought to have had a brain no bigger than a walnut This would have been very small for such a large animal, but it would also have been large enough to do what *Stegosaurus* needed it to do. Today, most scientists feel that *Stegosaurus*'s brain was three or four times bigger than the size of a walnut. Stegosaurs lived on earth for millions of years. They couldn't have done that if they'd had as little intelligence as people once thought. Some people think that *Stegosaurus* had a second brain in its hips. It did have a large nerve center there that helped to control its muscles. But it was not a real brain.

Scientists have found eggs that belonged to *Stegosaurus*, but they don't know if stegosaurs took care of their babies. Most scientists used to think stegosaurs were not smart enough to take care of babies. But then they found the skeleton of a young stegosaur with skeletons of several adults nearby. That could mean the adults were taking care of it—but it might not. The young stegosaur was about the size of a collie. It was probably big enough to keep up with a herd. It might have been on its own and had just found a herd to join. Or it might not have even been with those adults. We may never know for sure which is correct.

GLOSSARY

bellow . . . . a loud cry or roar

cycad . . . . a palmlike, cone-bearing evergreen plant with large leaves, or fronds

fern . . . . a flowerless, seedless plant with roots, stems, and long, thin leaves called fronds

graze . . . . to feed on growing plants

herd . . . . a number of animals of one kind living together

marsh . . . . an area of soft, wet, low-lying land with grassy vegetation

nesting grounds . . . an area set aside for laying eggs

FOR FURTHER READING

Benton, Michael. *Dinosaurs: An A–Z Guide.* New York: Derrydale Books, 1988.

Dixon, Dougal. *The Big Book of Dinosaurs.* New York: Derrydale Books, 1989.

Lindsay, William. *The Great Dinosaur Atlas.* New York: Dorling Kindersley, 1991.

Norman, David. *The Illustrated Encyclopedia of Dinosaurs.* New York: Crescent Books, 1985.

Riehecky, Janet. *Stegosaurus.* Mankato, MN: The Child's World, 1988.

Sattler, Helen Roney. *Stegosaurs: The Solar-Powered Dinosaurs.* New York: Lothrop, Lee & Shepard Books, 1992.

Stewart, Janet. *The Dinosaurs: A New Discovery.* Niagara Falls, NY: Hayes Publishing Co., 1989.

Storrs, Glenn W. *Stegosaurus.* New York: Kingfisher, 1994.

Sweat, Lynn. *The Smallest Stegosaurus.* New York: Viking, 1993.

INDEX